INCREDIBLE
SPORTS
RECORDS

FOOTBALL
RECORDS
BY ALLAN MOREY

BLASTOFF!
DISCOVERY

Bellwether Media • Minneapolis, MN

BLASTOFF! DISCOVERY

Blastoff! Discovery launches
a new mission: reading to learn.
Filled with facts and features,
each book offers you an exciting
new world to explore!

This edition first published in 2018 by Bellwether Media, Inc.

Library of Congress Cataloging-in-Publication Data

Names: Morey, Allan, author.
Title: Football Records / by Allan Morey.
Description: Minneapolis, MN : Bellwether Media, Inc., 2018. |
    Series: Blastoff! Discovery. Incredible Sports Records |
    Includes bibliographical references and index. | Audience:
    Age 7-13. | Audience: Grade 3 to 8.
Identifiers: LCCN 2017032154 (print) |
    LCCN 2017032983 (ebook) | ISBN 9781626177833
    (hardcover : alk. paper) | ISBN 9781618913135
    (pbk. : alk. paper) | ISBN 9781681034942 (ebook)
Subjects: LCSH: Football–Records–United States–Juvenile
    literature. | National Football League–Juvenile literature.
Classification: LCC GV955 (ebook) | LCC GV955 .M67 2018
    (print) | DDC 796.332/6406–dc23
LC record available at https://lccn.loc.gov/2017032154

Editor: Nathan Sommer   Designer: Steve Porter

Printed in the United States of America, North Mankato, MN.

TABLE OF CONTENTS

RECORD PASS

It is the last game of the 2013 season. Denver Broncos **quarterback** Peyton Manning lines up against the Oakland Raiders late in the first half. He passes to superstar **wide receiver** Demaryius Thomas. **Touchdown!**

The touchdown pass is Manning's record 55th of the season. His National Football League (NFL) record is one of many that have amazed fans over the years. Read on to learn about other incredible NFL records!

RECORD-BREAKING PLAYERS

Each NFL team plays just 16 times each season. Even with so few games, superstars can still rack up some amazing stats. This is what makes them some of the most talented and exciting players to ever play the game!

Many consider Jerry Rice to be the greatest football player ever. He had more catches and **receiving yards** than anyone in NFL history. But it is Rice's record 208 touchdowns scored that led so many to name him number one.

TREMENDOUS TOUCHDOWNS

Jerry Rice has the most career touchdowns, but running back LaDainian Tomlinson holds the single-season record. He scored 31 times in 2006!

CAREER TOUCHDOWNS
SCORED

Record: 208 touchdowns
Record holder: Jerry Rice
Year record was set: 2004
Former record holder: Jim Brown

ALL IN A SEASON

Smith might have the best career for a running back, but Eric Dickerson had the best single season. He rushed for 2,105 yards in 1984!

Running back

Emmitt Smith was nearly impossible to stop once he had the football. He ran for a record 18,355 **rushing** yards during his unforgettable 15-year career. His 164 career rushing touchdowns are also more than any other player.

CAREER RUSHING YARDS

Record: 18,355 yards
Record holder: Emmitt Smith
Year record was set: 2004
Former record holder:
Walter Payton

There is much debate over who is the best quarterback of all time. But Peyton Manning holds the most passing records. The icon threw more touchdowns than any other passer. His 71,940 career passing yards are an NFL record!

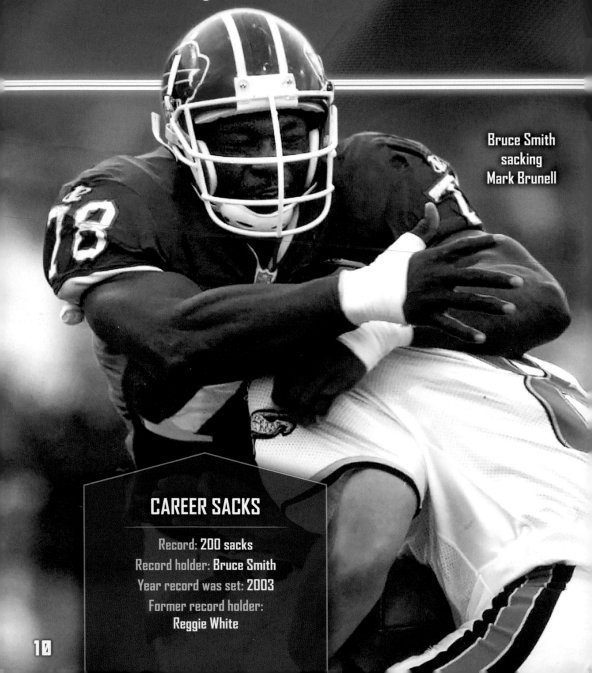

Bruce Smith was one of the NFL's most feared **defensive linemen**. He had 10 or more **sacks** in 13 of the 19 seasons he played. One year, Smith sacked opposing quarterbacks 19 times! He totaled a record 200 sacks during his NFL career.

Bruce Smith sacking Mark Brunell

CAREER SACKS

Record: 200 sacks
Record holder: Bruce Smith
Year record was set: 2003
Former record holder:
Reggie White

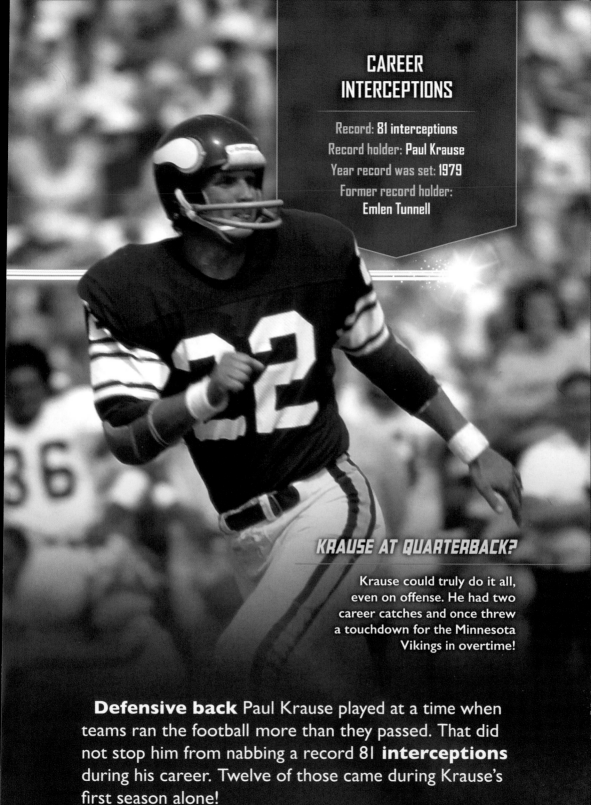

CAREER INTERCEPTIONS

Record: 81 interceptions
Record holder: Paul Krause
Year record was set: 1979
Former record holder:
Emlen Tunnell

KRAUSE AT QUARTERBACK?

Krause could truly do it all, even on offense. He had two career catches and once threw a touchdown for the Minnesota Vikings in overtime!

Defensive back Paul Krause played at a time when teams ran the football more than they passed. That did not stop him from nabbing a record 81 **interceptions** during his career. Twelve of those came during Krause's first season alone!

RECORD-BREAKING TEAMS

NFL teams need to play well on **offense** and **defense** to have a winning season. Teams can accomplish some pretty big things when they are coached well. Often these teams become dominating forces!

The 1972 Miami Dolphins are the only team in NFL history to have a perfect season. They won all 14 of their regular season games that year. Then they won both of their **playoff** games before finding victory at the Super Bowl!

FALLING SHORT

The New England Patriots came close to matching the Dolphins' feat in 2007. But they failed to win the Super Bowl!

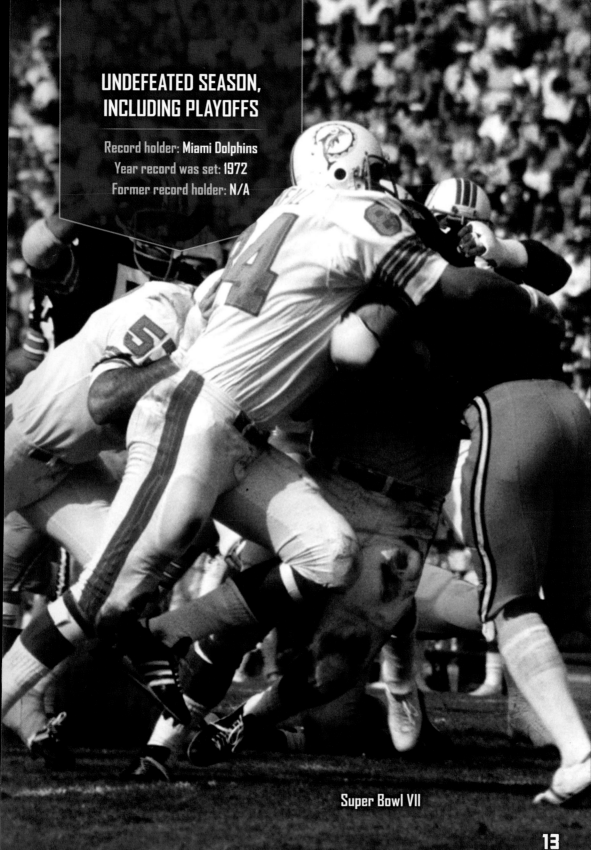

UNDEFEATED SEASON, INCLUDING PLAYOFFS

Record holder: Miami Dolphins
Year record was set: 1972
Former record holder: N/A

Super Bowl VII

The Super Bowl winner takes home the Lombardi Trophy. This trophy was named after iconic Packers head coach Vince Lombardi.

MOST NFL CHAMPIONSHIPS

Record: 13 championships
Record holder: Green Bay Packers
Year record was set: 2011
Former record holder:
Chicago Bears

Green Bay, Wisconsin has earned its nickname "Titletown." Its hometown team, the Packers, have won more NFL championships than any other team. They have been crowned champions 13 times since joining the league in 1921.

The Packers are part of one of the biggest **rivalries** in the NFL. Their rivalry with the Chicago Bears goes back to 1921! The teams have played around 200 times since then. They continue to play each other twice per season.

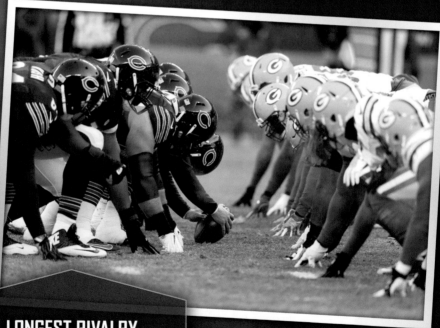

LONGEST RIVALRY

Record holders:
Green Bay Packers and
Chicago Bears
Year record was set:
started in 1921
Former record holders: N/A

SECOND PLACE

Like their rivals, the Bears have won their fair share of championships. They are right behind the Packers with nine titles!

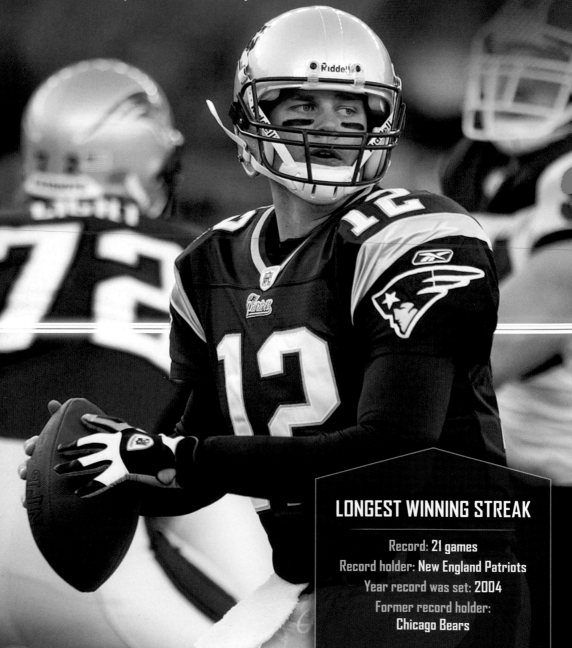

The New England Patriots have known how to win and win often. Led by star quarterback Tom Brady, they put together a winning **streak** of 21 games from 2003 to 2004. This record streak included two playoff wins and one Super Bowl victory.

LONGEST WINNING STREAK

Record: 21 games
Record holder: New England Patriots
Year record was set: 2004
Former record holder:
Chicago Bears

MOST GAMES LOST IN A SINGLE SEASON

Record: 16 losses
Record holder: Detroit Lions
Year record was set: 2008
Former record holder:
Tampa Bay Buccaneers

No team in NFL history has lost as many games as the 2008 Detroit Lions. The team lost every single one of its 16 games that season. It was so bad that its head coach and president were replaced before the next year!

RECORD-BREAKING GAMES

Every NFL game is action-packed. Both teams battle to see who can score the most points. Sometimes, it results in an unbelievable amount of points and yards. The most exciting games become record-breakers!

The Bears were a force in 1940. They proved it when they played the Washington Redskins in that year's championship game. The Bears easily beat the Redskins 73–0, the biggest **blowout** in NFL history!

BIGGEST BLOWOUT IN NFL HISTORY

Record: 73–0

Record holders: Chicago Bears and Washington Redskins

Year record was set: 1940

Former record holders:
Philadelphia Eagles and Cincinnati Reds

The Buffalo Bills trailed the Houston Oilers 35–3 at halftime on January 3, 1993. But then, the Bills flipped a switch and piled on the points! They ended up winning 41–38 in **overtime**. No team has ever had such a large comeback.

BIGGEST COMEBACK

Record: 32 points
Record holder: Buffalo Bills
Year record was set: 1993
Former record holder:
San Francisco 49ers

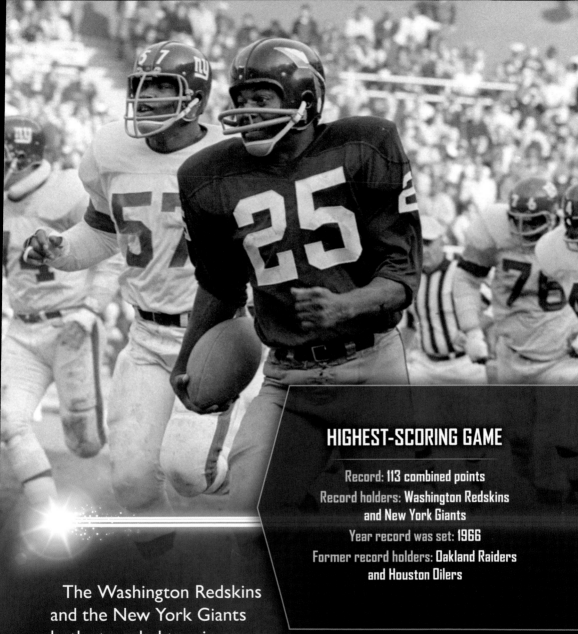

HIGHEST-SCORING GAME

Record: 113 combined points
Record holders: Washington Redskins and New York Giants
Year record was set: 1966
Former record holders: Oakland Raiders and Houston Oilers

The Washington Redskins and the New York Giants both struggled to win games in 1966. But on November 27, the teams scored a record 16 total touchdowns before the Redskins reached a 72–41 victory. It was the highest-scoring game in NFL history!

NO POINTS ALLOWED

Believe it or not, there have been more than 70 NFL games that ended in a 0–0 tie. The last one happened in 1943 between the Giants and Lions.

MOST RUSHING YARDS IN A GAME

Record: 296 yards
Record holder: Adrian Peterson
Year record was set: 2007
Former record holder:
Jamal Lewis

Running back Adrian Peterson carried the Minnesota Vikings to victory on November 4, 2007. He ran for an astounding 296 yards against the San Diego Chargers! Peterson averaged nearly 10 **yards per carry** as he ran away with the single-game rushing record.

Los Angeles Rams receiver Flipper Anderson could not be stopped on November 26, 1989. He had 15 catches for an amazing 336 yards that day. No one has had more receiving yards in a game since!

TOSSING THE FOOTBALL AROUND

Another Los Angeles Rams player holds the record for most passing yards in a game. Quarterback Norm Van Brocklin threw for 554 yards in 1951.

MOST RECEIVING YARDS IN A GAME

Record: 336 yards
Record holder: Flipper Anderson
Year record was set: 1989
Former record holder:
Stephone Paige

RECORD-BREAKING PLAYS

Football is a game of hard hits and exciting scores. Big plays often get fans up on their feet. Sometimes, they change the outcome of an entire game!

The Philadelphia Eagles were about to score against the Baltimore Ravens on November 23, 2008. Suddenly, Ravens defensive back Ed Reed intercepted a pass in his own end zone. He returned it a record 107 yards to score a touchdown.

LONGEST INTERCEPTION RETURN

Record: 107 yards
Record holder: Ed Reed
Year record was set: 2008
Former record holder:
Vencie Glenn

The Giants had the football on their 1-yard line during their December 24, 2011 game. Quarterback Eli Manning quickly passed to receiver Victor Cruz, who broke three tackles in a record-tying 99-yard score. Only 12 other pairs of quarterbacks and receivers have completed a 99-yard pass play.

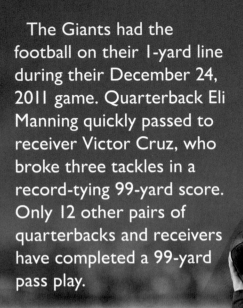

99-YARD PASS PLAY

The first 99-yard pass play happened in 1939. Redskins quarterback Frank Filchock threw 9 yards to running back Andy Farkas, who ran it 90 yards for a touchdown.

The Dallas Cowboys were trapped against their end zone on January 3, 1983. They handed running back Tony Dorsett the ball at the 1-yard line. Dorsett turned it into a historic play. He sprinted 99 yards for a touchdown and the NFL record.

LONGEST RUNNING PLAY

Record: 99 yards
Record holder: Tony Dorsett
Year record was set: 1983
Former record holders:
Andy Uram (1939) and
Bob Gage (1949)

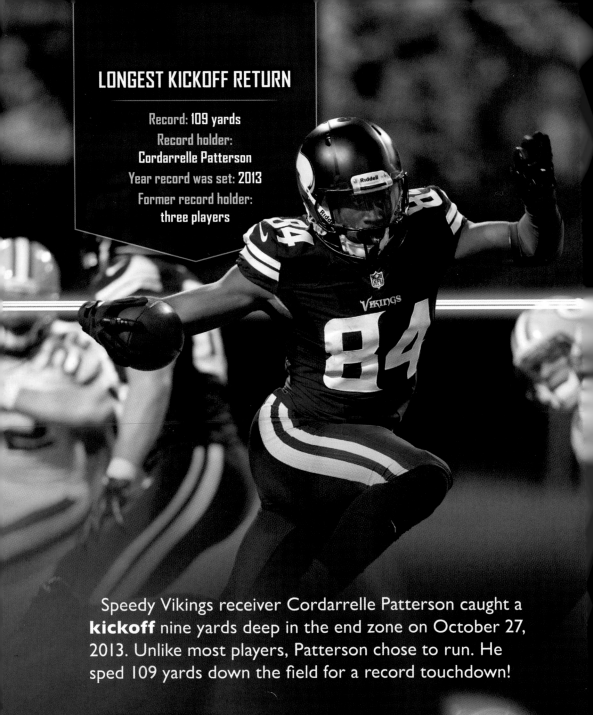

LONGEST KICKOFF RETURN

Record: 109 yards
Record holder:
Cordarrelle Patterson
Year record was set: 2013
Former record holder:
three players

Speedy Vikings receiver Cordarrelle Patterson caught a
kickoff nine yards deep in the end zone on October 27,
2013. Unlike most players, Patterson chose to run. He
sped 109 yards down the field for a record touchdown!

TAKING ONE BACK

When a team gets stopped from scoring, they punt
the football to the other team. Rams player Robert
Bailey returned a punt for a record 103 yards in 1994.

On December 6, 2013, Bronco Matt Prater proved why **kickers** are important in close games. He kicked a 64-yard **field goal** as the first half closed against the Tennessee Titans. It was the longest field goal in NFL history!

LONGEST FIELD GOAL

Record: 64 yards
Record holder: Matt Prater
Year record was set: 2013
Former record holders:
four players

GLOSSARY

blowout—a game in which one team wins by scoring many more points than the other team

defense—a group of players who try to stop the opposing team from scoring

defensive back—a defensive player whose main job is to keep wide receivers from catching the football; defensive backs are positioned behind all other players on defense.

defensive linemen—defensive players whose main job is to get to the quarterback and tackle rushers; defensive linemen crouch down in front of the football.

field goal—a score that occurs when a kicker kicks the football between the goal posts at one end of a football field; a field goal is worth 3 points.

interceptions—passes that are caught by a defensive player

kickers—players who specialize in kicking field goals and extra points; a kicker also kicks the football to the opposing team to start the game and after each score.

kickoff—when one team kicks the football to the other team to start play at the beginning of the game or after a score

offense—a group of players who try to move down the field and score

overtime—additional time played in a game to break a tie

playoff—a game played after the regular season is over; NFL playoff games determine which teams play in the Super Bowl.

quarterback—an offensive player whose main job is to throw and hand off the football

receiving yards—yards gained by a receiver on a pass play

rivalries—long-standing competitions between teams

running back—an offensive player whose main job is to take handoffs from the quarterback and run with the football

rushing—running with the football

sacks—plays in which a defensive player tackles the opposing quarterback for a loss of yards

streak—a series of events that happen one right after the other

touchdown—a score that occurs when a team crosses their opponent's end zone with the football; a touchdown is worth 6 points.

wide receiver—an offensive player whose main job is to catch passes from the quarterback

yards per carry—the number of yards a player averages with each run during a game

TO LEARN MORE

AT THE LIBRARY

Grace, Nicki Clausen, and Jeff Grace. *Football Teams by the Numbers.* Mankato, Minn.: Black Rabbit Books, 2018.

Hetrick, Hans. *Football's Record Breakers.* North Mankato, Minn.: Capstone Press, 2017.

Savage, Jeff. *Football Super Stats.* Minneapolis, Minn.: Lerner Publications, 2018.

ON THE WEB

Learning more about football records is as easy as 1, 2, 3.

1. Go to www.factsurfer.com.

2. Enter "football records" into the search box.

3. Click the "Surf" button and you will see a list of related web sites.

With factsurfer.com, finding more information is just a click away.

INDEX

The images in this book are reproduced through the courtesy of: Focus On Sport/ Contributor/ Getty Images, front cover (Jerry Rice), pp. 8, 27; EFKS, front cover (stadium); piaharrisphotography, p. 2 (fabric background); David Lee, p. 3 (football); Waj, p. 3 (metal background); Ezra Shaw/ Staff/ Getty Images, pp. 4-5; G. Newman Lowrance/ AP Images, pp. 6-7; Dustin Bradford/ Stringer/ Getty Images, p. 9; Kevin Rivoli/ AP Images, p. 10; Tony Tomsic/ AP Images, p. 11; Nate Fine/ Contributor/ Getty Images, pp. 12-13; David J. Phillip/ AP Images, pp. 14-15; Paul Spinelli/ AP Images, p. 15 (inset); Tomasso DeRosa/ AP Images, p. 16; Mike Roemer/ AP Images, p. 17; Bettmann/ Contributor/ Getty Images, pp. 18-19, 21; John Hickey/ AP Images, p. 20; Bryan C Singer/ Icon SMI/ Newscom, p. 22; Otto Greule Jr/ Stringer/ Getty Images, p. 23; The Washington Post/ Contributor/ Getty Images, pp. 24-25; Jim McIsaac/ Contributor/ Getty Images, p. 26; David Stluka/ AP Images, p. 28; Justin Edmonds/ Stringer/ Getty Images, p. 29.